GET IT RIGHT
WITH YOUR
CUSTOMERS & EMPLOYEES

GET IT RIGHT
WITH YOUR CUSTOMERS & EMPLOYEES

Ahmed Shehu Awak, PhD

AuthorHouse™ UK Ltd.
1663 Liberty Drive
Bloomington, IN 47403 USA
www.authorhouse.co.uk
Phone: 0800.197.4150

Published by AuthorHouse 05/30/2013

ISBN: 978-1-4817-9721-4 (sc)
ISBN: 978-1-4817-9722-1 (e)

Dedication

Late Ambassador Shehu Awak, OFR. May Aljannah firdausi be your residence, ameen.

Preface

This is a general business book that focuses on the attitudes and perceptions of the people in charge of other people in places of work—either public or private.

The book provides an insight into the activities and lives of people who run businesses, whether Government or privately owned, their priorities in running the outfits and how they view the outfits they manage.

A lot of practical examples were made use of in order to bring to light the nature of managers and the reaction of customers towards the services they receive from various outfits—banks, hotels, restaurants, hospitals, barber shops, auto-mechanic garages and a lot more.

This book further provides insight into the nature of customers, employees and managers. It also helps you shape your perception on how you should run your outfit—from a barber shop to a large corporation, and be a winner and a natural at what you do. It cuts across all borders of industry. The president of Toyota could pick a thing or two, likewise the auto-mechanic garage and all others.

Acknowledgement

To the mothers: Mami Hauwa, (Biological), Mami—Aisha Awak, Beloved Adda (Justice Zainab Bulkachuwa) Mami-Hannatu, Mami-Dija, Wawu, Mami-Tom-tom,mama-kembu Mama-Hajia K.O, Mama—Hajia—Binta Maisango, Mama Kelo, Mami Hardawa, Mama Fadila—Hamza—Katsina, Momi—Sa'adatu—Y—Ibn—Mohammed, Mama—Prof. Gambo—Laraba, Babba—Iya—Abubakar, Maman Jamilu, Mama Farida—Yaya—Abubakar, Mama Zainab—Ahmed, Mama Edna—Jimeta, Mama Aisha—Pindar,mama-hannatu-adamu hussaini,mama-mariya-hassan-mohammed-Santana, mama-Kubli-Yarima-Abdullahi,mama-Fatima-Ahmed-Adamu, mama-mary-awak—you will always be cherished . . . .

Madam Thessy, thanks again. My author house family, thanks again for a beautiful job. All family members and friends, thank you for all the love and support.

Acknowledgement

Contents

Chapter Five

Chapter Six

Chapter One

The Customer

Everyone is a customer somewhere, somehow. A barber is a customer at the Bank; the banker is a customer at the barber's shop. A medical doctor is a customer at a grocery store; an ill carpenter is a customer at the doctor's clinic. A police man is a customer at a music store and so goes the circle, entwined around life itself.

People hardly can do without each other. People need people to provide so many important services in their lives to make it complete. A person cannot provide everything he/she needs in life, thus the need to find someone that provides such service. A gardener, carpenter, plumber, barber, policeman, grocery provider, doctor, an architect, a mechanic and so many other services required by people.

It is evident that we all need a lot while alive to make life convenient, which is the root for being in need of each other's services. This is the individual perception of a customer. Even countries at large are customers to each other. A lot of the developed nations in the world patronize the under-developed and developing countries for so many natural resources that they use to manufacture so many products. The under-developed and developing countries in return, buy so many products they need from the developed nations in order to satisfy their needs. For instance, Nigeria does not have the technological know-how to manufacture cars, but you find all brands of cars in the country; Honda,

Toyota, Nissan, Ford, Mercedes, Chevrolet and a lot of others. Meanwhile, Nigeria is endowed with steel that is used in the manufacture of cars. Then within the manufacturing circle of cars, you find out that the brake pads of a certain car are manufactured in a different country, the windscreen, shock absorber, tire and so many other components are manufactured by different companies, not by the company that manufactures the car in a certain country.

In essence, people need people for so many services, not only within their environment, but all over the world at large.

The concept of being a customer or having a customer can be limited to your environment and also to the whole world. E-bay, Amazon and a lot of other product servicing companies have customers all over the world. This is due to the marketing channel they use; the internet.

This provides a platform for so many people all over the world to gain access to their services. This has made the whole world their customer base.

It is not every business outfit that can use and apply the internet as a marketing channel for its products or services. For instance, if you own a barber shop and you advertise it on the internet, it may be almost impossible for Mr. Adam who resides in Nigeria to access it while it is in U.K. This is a sort of border line on the customer base of your business outfit. You can only tap a customer base that is convenient to the proximity of the nature of your business.

It is very important to consider the nature of your business or the business you intend to establish in order to identify your type of customer base and the channels you will choose to reach out to them. This will help you have a better focus on your business and customers and how to serve them most efficiently and effectively.

The world as it exists now is more or less a global village. Anybody could be anybody's customer depending on the need that arises. The limit depends on your service specialty, which makes or creates a global customer base for some services and none for others. The auto-industry for instance, and even the medical industry, has automatic global outreach than the retail industry or the tailoring industry. The automotive and medical customer base could be unlimited due to its specialization, while a retail superstore or a tailor can only have a limited coverage.

People could travel far and wide for a highly specialized surgery to a country where proficiency is high and recognized all over the world, but hardly would a person travel from one country to another just to get his pants done by a certain tailor. It is hoped that the concept behind the word "customer" has a clearer picture to you now. However, emphasis will be laid on business outfits with a limitation to customer base than global, which is not to say the global outfit would be neglected in the book.

The Customer Matrix

Mr. Nas was on a business trip to a foreign country, from his home country. He had a few days off before his next appointment, and was experiencing some symptoms he was not used to, so he decided to visit one of the hospitals there.

He got to the hospital, looked around and was finally able to locate an enquiry desk. He asked on how he could see a doctor and was told the procedure. He went through it and was finally seated in front of the doctor. After a question and answer session between them, the doctor suggested that he should be admitted for some examination. Mr. Nas politely declined that he does not feel so bad enough to be admitted, because it will affect his business appointment. He thanked the doctor and left the hospital.

Immediately he left, he took a cab and while conversing with the cab guy, he asked him if he knew a good hospital around. The cab guy made a quick detour and took him to another hospital. He thanked and paid him, then walked into the hospital.

As he walked in, a smart looking young man approached him, greeted him warmly, welcomed him to the hospital and asked him how he could be of service. Mr. Nas briefly told him why he was there and what he wanted. The young man found a comfortable couch for him, then took off and was back a few minutes later, collected Mr. Nas' details, went away again and came back then ushered Mr. Nas into a doctor's office.

The doctor stood up, greeted Mr. Nas warmly, with an affectionate smile and said to Mr. Nas "you are a double guest, first you are a guest in our country and then at our hospital, we treat double guests with double service speed".

Seated and smiling and listening to Mr. Nas' complaints, he put him to bed in the office, examined him and ordered some tests be carried out immediately. The young man took

Mr. Nas out to hospital laboratory, where blood sample was collected and he was urged to come in the next day early in the morning before having his breakfast.

The next morning, Mr. Nas was there at the scheduled time and was received by the same young man who welcomed him the previous day.

The young man now took him for some further tests and examinations. After that, he took him to a restaurant at the hospital and asked him to order for his breakfast. He then left and came back a while later and asked him if 4pm would be convenient for him to see the doctor again. Mr. Nas agreed with the timing and left.

At 4pm prompt, Mr. Nas was back and received by the same young man, who whisked him straight to the doctor's office. The doctor welcomed him again and discussed the outcome of all the examination carried out on him. He then wrote a prescription for him and wished him a happy time while still in the country.

The young man took Mr. Nas to the hospital's pharmacy where he was able to purchase his medication. The young man thanked him for visiting their hospital and gave him his business card and pleaded that Mr. Nas could call anytime in case he needed anything.

Mr. Nas thanked the young man and left, pleased with services he had received.

Hmm wow! Okay let's move on to Mr. Ray's experience.

Mr. Ray desperately needed to open a current account so that he could be issuing cheques to some of his vendors, instead of always visiting his microfinance bank to withdraw from his savings account. This time around, he selected two of the leading banks in his country, for the current account opening.

He collected the application forms from both banks, completed all the requirements needed and submitted it back, with a single and simple reason; "the first bank to finish opening the account and making available the cheque book will be the bank I will use", decided Mr. Ray.

After a week, he visited both banks to find out if the account was ready for use. The first bank apologized for the delay in processing his cheque book and the second bank too.

The second bank however, kept calling Mr. Ray after every two days and kept apologizing and promising him it will be ready within a short while. Mr. Ray, furious and impatient kept cursing whenever the second bank called. The first bank never called to update Mr. Ray however.

Finally, the second bank called again, apologized profusely and received a lot of insults from Mr. Ray politely. His cheque book was ready. Mr. Ray went to the bank, collected the cheque book and made some deposit into the account, cursing the employees for all the delay and walked out.

Two weeks later, the first bank called and told Mr. Ray his cheque book was ready. Mr. Ray told them to keep it and use probably for making fire or something and slammed the phone on the caller.

The call came in again insisting Mr. Ray pick it up and make a deposit. "Go to hell!" replied Ray and cut the line.

Give it up; the first bank has lost Mr. Ray's account to the second bank.

Let's peep into Mr. Adam's experience.

Mr. Adam went out seeking to buy a particular brand of car. He visited various used car dealers but did not find what he actually wanted because what he saw had one or two missing accessories that he really cherished to have in the car.

So he continued his search, visiting more dealer outlets, because he could not afford a brand new one. He met a particular dealer that was extremely nice to him, who showed him the exact model he was looking for, but unfortunately it has been bought and the buyer went to get the money and on his way back.

Adam was sad. The dealer kindly asked Adam if he could afford to wait for five days, he will bring another one exactly, because it was on its way to be delivered to him. Brightly, Adam accepted and even paid for the car so that he does not even spend from the budgeted car money.

The dealer wrote a payment receipt and issued Adam. Adam left excitedly waiting to receive a call from his new dealer friend within the next four or five days.

Five days later, Adam called and was disappointed because his car had not arrived. The dealer apologized and promised Adam the car will be on ground by the next day. This issue lingered for the next five months. Finally, the car arrived and Adam went and picked it up. Adam asked his dealer friend what really went wrong. The dealer simply said it was circumstances beyond his control. Adam smiled and simply said "I don't think I could ever refer someone else to your company" then left. Three weeks later, Adam brought a friend to buy a car there, but without payment until the car arrives. Hmm, what a heart Adam has got. Adam's dealer friend could not make the particular car available, so Adam and his friend ended up buying, elsewhere. Adam never stopped patronizing his dealer friend though.

Customer Matrix Dissection

The most similar people in the world, we could say are the identical twins, yet they also have a lot of differences in behavior and attitude.

Hence, people are never the same in the way they perceive or react to other people and situations. If you take a look at the world entirely, you would find out that there are a lot of different ethnicities all over with different religions, cultures, topography and so many other elements that may influence behavior and attitude.

These factors and elements most certainly play a great role in understanding people. Let's take the most primary unit for instance, a family of seven: The father, mother and five kids. The father may probably be an introvert who likes to spend his time reading the dailies whenever he is free, hates going out and likes it nice and quite all the time. The mother, very extroverted and outgoing, likes throwing picnics over the weekends inviting friends and relatives and hardly appreciating dull moments. The five kids; one quite, one hot tempered, one calm and friendly, one very impatient and the fifth calm but hot tempered and an extrovert.

You see from the combination of their different attitudes and behavior, one would wonder how the amalgamation of all of them would be under the same roof.

Simple, as they live together, everyone notices and absorbs the other's attitudes and behavior and finds a way of accepting, coping and enjoying each other's love and company.

Now these rules apply directly to the business world too. Our customers cannot all be the same in behavior and attitude. The business world referred to extends to all kinds of work; government officials, bankers, air hostesses, barbers, technicians, doctors etc.

When dealing with people, most especially as customers, you have to be able to read in between the lines so as to cope and tame different personalities.

Some customers may turn out to be:

(i) Quite, patient and friendly
(ii) Quite, impatient and unfriendly
(iii) Quite, patient but unfriendly
(iv) Aggressive, patient and friendly
(v) Aggressive, impatient and unfriendly
(vi) Aggressive, patient and unfriendly
(vii) Quite, watchful and loyal
(viii) Quite, watchful and disloyal

(ix) Unpredictable minds—that is, a complex combination of the above factors.

These are basically a primary mix or classification of different personalities you tend to encounter in your daily business life, whether as hospital patients, legal clients, in government offices, supermarkets, hotels, bank customers etc.

Looking back at Mr. Nas' experience at the first and second hospital while he was on his business trip, one would surely feel he is the "quite, watchful, patient, friendly and disloyal" type, because of the manner he handled his hospital experience. Now, chances are, if Mr. Nas is to recommend a hospital for you in that country, he will simply recommend the second one that favored him and discourage you from visiting the first one. This will obviously be based on a lot of factors, most importantly the vendor reception differences.

Taking into account of Mr. Ray's experience with opening of his current bank account, some would say he is the "aggressive, impatient and unfriendly" type, others would say he is the "aggressive, impatient and loyal" type. The combination of the character variables may not necessarily be exactly as outlined earlier. The purpose was to simply bring to focus how volatile and different people could be.

Despite the fact that Mr. Ray was troublesome before he finally got his cheque book from the second bank, he is most certainly to recommend the second bank than the first who never called him and followed up on his account opening.

For Mr. Adam, who after all the waiting for his car to arrive for months, all the disappointments he got from his car dealer, still kept patronizing the dealer could simply be referred to as the "quite, patient, friendly, watchful and loyal" type of customer.

You may encounter people with a different combination of the customer mix and it will be left to you to be able to patiently and effectively sort out the kind of personality you are handling or dealing with.

You have to always watch out for the "customer bullet". Do not always assume that all people are nice and the same. The way a certain customer may treat you might even make you feel sick or depressed, so always wear a customer bullet proof jacket and be ready to tame.

Chapter Two

The Business

Anything you are engaged in, permanently or periodically, that provides you with financial benefits, that you use to make ends meet can be looked upon as your business.

Of course people engage in different activities in life; for one reason or the other, but most people have a primary activity termed as work, to make ends meet.

You may be a university student studying law or sociology. That is not yet your business, but when you graduate and seek employment in a law firm or start your own independent firm, then that is your business because you will seek to make ends meet through whatever you make out of it.

In essence, not every activity is a business. You could be a medical doctor and belong to a fitness club or an architect and belong to a biker's club. You engage in a fitness club or a biker's club to derive a different need, not to make ends meet. Rather you may have to contribute to being part of that activity by paying daily, weekly, monthly or annual dues as the case may be.

You could be engaged in ten different activities, but the one(s) that brings in income is your business.

Business People

The intention of people to be really involved in business varies all over the world. The motives, intentions and objectives of why some people go into business and succeed, while others go into it and fail is a complex issue with different factors in almost every country.

A business that could fail in one country may succeed in another country, due to the different forces of success and failure in the respective countries.

We could categorize people being in business or going into business as such:

(i) **Necessity business people:**
These people often engage into a business venture due to lack of wage employment or any other opportunity to make ends meet.

(ii) **Opportunity business people:**
These people are in business not because they lack other opportunities, but because they sense, see or perceive an opportunity or opportunities to exploit and make a living.

(iii) **Natural business people**
These are usually people born with one or more creative talent and derive pleasure exploiting the talent while earning a living through it.

(iv) **Pleasure business people**
These are people that are in a business simply for the pleasure of providing a certain service for the community, even though profitable, but the profit is a secondary motive. These people usually have a lot of financial muscle and don't really bother about the day to day affairs of business, which is usually taken care of by other people.

Now this categorization is by no means the final assessment of business people. A person may start as a necessity business man, become highly successful and convert into a pleasure business man.

As a business person, whatever category you happen to belong, you can always succeed with the adoption of the right business ethics.

The Profit Syndrome

There is a certain hospital with a lot of international patients all over the world. Yes, they are actually good in terms of medical services and personnel, I must admit, but there is more than meets the eye.

Mr. Gee visited the hospital once concerning a certain ailment he had. He was treated well and he left happily.

Being a frequent visitor to the country, a few months later, he decided to visit another different hospital for the same ailment that had relapsed.

He saw the specialized doctor and was asked to go through some medical examination just like the former hospital, but less.

After collecting the results and treatment prescription from the doctor, he simply asked the doctor why the tests were few unlike another hospital he visited and the doctor simply told him that the tests carried out were all that was needed, any other was a waste of money.

Mr. Gee now realized that the other hospital only did all in order to maximize cash coming into the hospital, since he didn't know the medical processes. Hmm, so much for profit maximization.

Okay, enough said about Mr. Gee's encounter.

Mr. Loot as fondly called by friends and family, has been a regular and consistent guest at a particular hotel whenever he travels to do business in a certain country. He is so used to the hotel and its staff that he feels like a stakeholder there, most times even giving advice on how some issues should be looked into.

Now, on this particular trip, when he arrived, the hotel had been booked completely by a particular organization having a workshop of some sort. Mr. Loot had no option, but to search for another nice and affordable hotel like the one he is used to.

After a couple of hours of going round and checking out different hotels, he settled for one that was quite favorable to his budget. He was received well and treated as nicely as he had hoped, but even better.

The manager asked him how long his stay would be. "About ten to twelve days" replied Mr. Loot.

"Okay sir", answered the manager and said to Mr. Loot; "for our guests staying that long, we have a package for you. For every four days you spend, the fifth day is free, free breakfast every morning and 50 percent discount on all laundry.

The manager could not help but notice the surprise on Mr. Loot's face. "If there is anything I can do for you, please don't hesitate to call me anytime and I hope you enjoy your stay with us."

Mr. Loot thanked him and assured the manager he is already enjoying the stay, LOL!!

So why have they not been giving me such nice discounts and incentives after over five years of patronage?, thought Mr. Loot, aloud in his room.

That was the end of the road for his old hotel. He never went there again, they never called him. After he returned home, the manager of his new hotel sent him a text message to find out if he had arrived home safely. He replied him happily and thanked him for the concern. Once in a while, he receives a text message from the manager wishing him well.

Mr. Loot kept wondering why he never sampled other hotels long ago. From then onwards, he sampled even the business partners he buys goods from.

There is this small time business man that is into selling potato chips. He makes it at home and distributes to shops, pubs and so on. A few days later, he would go round and collect the cash proceeds, deduct some percentage of the profits along with the working capital and take some minute part of the profits for savings at the bank.

He kept on running his business and taking some savings to the bank for a very long time, years actually. He was never aware that his bank manager had been following the records of his savings account.

On this particular day, he came into the bank as usual to make a deposit into his savings account. The manager waited until he was done, then greeted him and invited him into his office for a chat. He was actually surprised at the invitation.

"I have been monitoring your account for the past two years now and your lodgments have been consistent every week for these two years. The deposit is always small but it is always there—and that's the kind of people we really value here and always willing to lend a helping hand. So what is it that you do Mr.?" . . . . "El-guys, Mr. El-guys" replied the manager.

"I make potato and plantain chips with hot sauce and distribute to a few shops and pubs," said Mr. El-guys.

"That's very good", replied the Bank manager. "If you have access to more capital it means you can expand your service points and earn more right?" "Yes, absolutely" replied Mr. El-guys excitedly.

"Next week when coming to the bank, please write an application for the amount you need for expansion and I will make sure you get it". "Thank you so much!" replied a happy and bubbling El-guys.

The following week, Mr. El-guys submitted his proposal to the manager and two weeks later, his account was credited with exactly what he requested for; with a leverage of six months free interest on the loan to enable him set up his business plan properly. "Hmmm . . . . I wish all bank managers and banks could be like that".

Mr. El-guys employed helping hands for expansion. He began servicing 50% of his city and in a little while, he had to hire a few more people because of demand. He kept growing and the deposits at the bank kept multiplying in ten folds. He finally had to ditch his gardening job to focus full time on his self owned business that now pays his bills.

Mr. Haidar and his wife watched a movie at home before going to bed, at about 12am. Suddenly his wife woke him up at 4am complaining about some severe stomach upset.

He hurriedly took her into the car and off they were to a hospital. The doctor on call came and examined her, wrote some stuff on a sheet of paper and said to Mr. Haidar that he was admitting her for some stomach complications. "Don't you have some sort of tests to conduct before admission, you admit just like that?" We shall conduct all tests tomorrow morning sir, replied the doctor". No I do not accept, please give her a pain relieving injection and let us go home, said Mr. Haidar. Well if you insist, answered the doctor. "Yes I do please" determined Haidar replied.

She was given a pain relieving injection and they defied the admission and went home. In the morning Mr. Haidar took his wife to another different hospital where she was examined and tests were carried out properly and there was not any need for admission. Hmmm . . . . Mr. Haidar later found out that the doctors had a certain percentage of the admission fees paid, which motivated them to admit patients unnecessarily and make money for themselves and the hospitals. How horrible a profit syndrome that is . . . .

PROFIT SYNDROME ANALYZED

Looking back at the stories of Mr. Gee and his two hospitals, Mr. Loot and his two hotels, Mr. El-guys and his bank manager and Mr. Haidar and his wife's escapade, we can't help but realize that people have different motives and perceptions of running a business of any sort.

The first hospital Mr. Gee went to was strictly money/profit oriented even though giving you the service. The second hospital was profit oriented alright, but sensitive to the customer's/patient's needs.

The first hotel Mr. Loot had been patronizing for over 5 years was sensitive only to its pocket, while his new found hotel actually had incentives that made customers feel appreciated and cared for, to the extent of calling their customers when they arrived back home and periodically keeping in touch with them.

For Mr. El-guys, he was completely unaware of the customer-care-policy of the bank he patronizes and it came to him as a nice surprise. Mr. Haidar was terribly shocked at the extent people could go to make profits at other people's expense.

People usually run businesses with different motives, as we have seen here.

Consider these points:

1. It is usually a bad business ethic to put your business "FIRST ALWAYS", without giving consideration to the factor that keeps your business alive—"the customer, your customer".
2. You tend to lose track of the customer's sensitivity for yours only.
3. While you are busy romancing your own side of the objectives, the customer may become displeased or realize that your competitor(s) care for him/her better than you do.
4. How you treat and handle your customers is a direct image and impression of your business outfit.
5. Avoid the knack for quick profits, for it makes you dissatisfy a lot of customer issues.
6. Caring for your customers will not erode your profits, rather it will only increase it.
7. Consider your business dead without a satisfied customer, hence the need to have a customer-satisfying-service and policy.
8. Do not push your discount margin too low to your distributors to the extent of causing dissatisfaction, because they will all switch to your competitor. That is if you are in the distribution service.
9. If your motivation in business is strictly "profits", the tendencies of failure is higher.

10. "Passion" is usually an important ingredient in succeeding in your business, because it helps give you drive and vision.
11. Understanding and identifying your target market will help you know how to treat your business.

There is this Bank I went to make some deposit into a friend's account. When I drove to the bank, being my first time there, the first thing I noticed was the inadequate parking space. They had only four car space for customers. The building looked good and befitting for a bank anyway, but when I walked into the banking hall, I noticed something in common with the staff and the customers; they were all sweating and fanning themselves with some paper or envelope or any stuff they could use.

So I filled in a deposit slip and joined the queue that was not too long anyway. I looked all around and noticed that not a single friendly smile was in the air by the staff or customers. Everyone looked moody and too serious. The staff wanted to get over with the customers and vice versa.

This is not the aura of a banking hall, where on entrance you will have a sense of calm, friendliness, security and a temperate atmosphere that you can enjoy with the CNN,ALJAZEERAH or BBC updating you on what the world is into.

It got to my turn and I handed over my deposit slip and the cash. I could see the young teller sweating and counting my cash. I simply asked him why the banking hall was so hot and what was wrong with their air conditioning. In a single wave that showed frustration and depression, he sighed and was like forget this damn bank.

Now this is a total neglect of the ethics of customer service and employees too. It may not come as a surprise if these young tellers keep having shortages when it is time to balance their books at the end of the working day. The environment is not work friendly and customer accommodating in any sense.

The next time I had to make a cash deposit for him, I asked him for a different account in another bank entirely, because what rushed into my mind was the problem of finding a place to park first, then the heat I will encounter inside the banking hall with some staff and customers being forced to perspire and you take in the smell because you have no choice. This impression will last a long while and will not ever want to visit any of their branches. First impressions they say lasts longer . . . .

I think I am the quite, watchful and of course the disloyal type. If you want my loyalty as a customer, do the right thing . . . .

Travelling through four states in Nigeria, kaybee had some ear problem and decided to make a stop over to see a doctor in one of the four states.

Kaybee asked around for a good "ENT" clinic and was directed to the best.

He had difficulty locating the clinic from the description, but finally did after a lot of guidance.

He got in and asked the receptionist if the doctor was available. "yes he will be around in a short while", the lady answered, so kaybee did all the necessary registration and all, sat down and waited for the doctor's arrival. He noticed a lot of flaws in the clinic. Really bad furniture, dirty drapes and inattentive looking nurses going up and down.

Kaybee noticed that there were other professional specialist doctors too. He asked the receptionist who confirmed to him that as far as this town is concerned; all the best specialists are here in this hospital.

After his consultation with the doctor, which he was satisfied, he decided to pinpoint all the flaws of the hospital to the doctor, from the poor and small sign board down to the bad furnishing and incompetent looking nurses.

The doctor surprised at kaybee's knowledge of a business outfit really thanked him and promised to heed to all the relevant changes to be made.

It is not enough to be the best at what you do or offer, then neglect the condition, environment and quality of services you offer simply because you are competent. Give the right services to your customers.

Chapter Three

Organizing your business outfit

> "You are a customer somewhere too, so treat your customers how you would like to be treated elsewhere".
>
> —Ahmed Shehu Awak, PhD

Two brothers graduated from the university with good grades. The first, "Dado" by name and the second, "Gidado", fondly called "Lex" by family and friends.

Dado and Lex both studied business administration.

They approached their father for loans to start up their business outfits. After a lengthy discussion with their dad, he agreed to loan them enough capital to start their businesses, but urged them to do a thorough feasibility study and come up with a good business plan.

Dado and Lex went ahead and did a thorough business plan and submitted a copy each to their father.

Impressed, their father released funds to them.

Dado's business proposal was on a restaurant while Lex's was on an ultra modern fitness gym.

With a well laid business plan and capital to execute, Dado and Lex went to work.

Dado followed his business plan religiously and did all the necessary and important things needed to be done. He was almost there for a successful outfit.

Lex on the other hand had other plans in mind. "Look" he said to himself, "I can succeed with less equipment for the gym and few staff so that I can cut down expenses of running the business and make more profits".

"Yes that is exactly what I am going to do, I am a business expert and I will use the remaining capital for other stuff," smiled Lex confidently.

Instead of purchasing the required number of equipment, Lex cut it by 50%. In fact he slashed the whole business plan into two. He simply, ignored the required capacity needed and felt the 50% will do. He went ahead and set up the business and lavished the remaining 50% capital on his lifelong hobby, he formed a pleasure music band for himself and friends.

Meanwhile, Dado set up his outfit well and was ready to open his doors to the public. The first day was completely free and a lot of people came in to have a taste of his menu. You know people like new things, most especially when it is offered for free. Dado had a full and fulfilled opening of his restaurant and it was a real success. Business has commenced.

A week later Lex opened his gym and people were happy about a fitness center in the neighborhood. Yes, the place was filled up with people alright, but people had to take turns due to inadequate equipment.

"That's alright, thought Lex, it is because everyone is eager today, when they start paying by tomorrow it will not be this jam packed.

For the next couple of weeks, Lex enjoyed a jam packed patronage. Barely into the second month, customers turned scanty.

Worried, Lex asked the two staff he employed what was happening. "Some of them are fed up of having to queue up in order to have access to our equipment, so they are dropping off gradually" replied one of the staff. Sir, we need more equipment and more staff to be able to maintain and retain customers". I shall look into that, for now just try and manage them with the available equipment before I bring in more," which he never did.

Now his business took a slow turn. The reason was all the customers were not sure of when to come over and meet the equipment free or with few people. The business remained on that level. Lex had to get a job to compliment his earnings in the long run.

Dado's restaurant was doing very well and he opened additional outlets in two other parts of the city. He was a success story and a good employer of labor.

Lex cut corners and failed or ignored the customer-sensitivity of his business outfit, which was a one sided business operation. He focused more on himself and pushed the customers' needs to the edge.

Failure, stagnation or decline of a business is always the result of ignoring your customers' needs when in business or setting up one, in most cases.

Most times when organizing your business outfit, the ultimate priority should be how to serve your customers best. Do not apply any method or technique or ways that would compromise the satisfaction of a customer. If you visit a hospital, hotel, barber's shop, bank or any other business outfit and you happen to be displeased with one or more of the services rendered, think about your own outfit and put yourself in a customer's shoe. Ask yourself "If I were a customer here, what is it here that I will be displeased with?" That will always help you keep check of your services to your customers, because really, you are nothing without them.

There should not be any compromise about your outfit, because any flaw(s) will be noticed by your customers and that could send away one or two or more without you knowing or noticing, until it is quite too late.

The reception received by your customers will keep them coming or leaving and no business owner would want the customers leaving, because it means something is not right about your services.

IT'S ALL ABOUT YOU AS A LEADER

> "Do not just employ people and go to sleep, be part of the work, you have the best vision for the outfit, make it a reality".
>
> —Ahmed Shehu Awak, PhD

It is not enough to set up a business outfit and just let go. Most times, you must have envisaged how, what and where you want the business to be and its potential future.

Letting go or completely delegating it out may limit the vision you have for it. You may or could employ a competent management team to overlook its welfare, but still have inputs here and there so as to realize your ultimate vision for the business. This of course is subject to the size of the business. Some businesses do not need outsourcing a management team due to its nature and size while others do, so it is strictly dependent on what you are into as a business.

Leadership quotes retrieved from Yoskovitz (2007):

> **"The very essence of leadership is that you have to have vision. You can't blow an uncertain trumpet"—Theodore M. Hesburgh**
>
> **"Don't tell people how to do things, tell them what to do and let them surprise you with results."—George S. Patton**

> **"Delegating works, provided the one leading works too"**
>
> **—Robert Half**

There are certain traits of personality a leader should have or be able to grasp, in order to lead successfully or at least be part of a progressive outfit. These basic skills could be outlined as follows:

1. **You have to be able to lead by example:**
   You can't be a "missing in action" leader, never being around and incapable of getting your hands dirty. One of the best ways is to lead by example—pitching in where needed, lending a helping hand, and making sure that the work you do is clearly understood by your team that is your staff.

2. **You have to Delegate:**
   It is impossible to do everything, you can't. An effective leader needs to be able to delegate efficiently. The key to delegating successfully is giving employees ownership of the work you assign them. They can't just feel like they own the work, they really have to.

3. **You have to have passion:**
   A leader without passion can't be a successful one, because passion drives a lot, and you can inspire so much in others through your own passion and enthusiasm. Without passion, you may end up being a paper pusher, a task-maker or a government employee. That does not mean you have to be constantly cheery and playful, no, it means you have

to believe in what you are doing and what your outfit is doing, whatever it is—barber's shop, hospital, car manufacturer etc.

4. **You have to be organized:**
   A disorganized leader is not leading; he is chasing his own tail. Disorganization breeds nothing but more disorganization. If you are messy, always in a rush—: whatever and however you are, your team will be affected and also be like that, almost or completely. When you are organized, you will be much more productive and so will everyone else.

5. **You have to take ownership and responsibility:**
   Although you have delegated most of the work and truly given your team ownership, you also have to take ownership and responsibility at all times. Your team has to know you will be there for them through the thick and thin. That does not also mean you absolve people from making mistakes or ignore crappy work/effort but it does mean you take responsibility for the big picture: achieving the organization's objectives by satisfying the customer's needs and aspirations.

6. **You have to communicate effectively:**
   It is a known fact that great leaders are always great communicators. There are certain points of communication that many people forget, for example, letting or making your employees aware of how their work matters in the bigger picture of the outfit.

Communicating success is also something leaders forget to do. People need affirmation. They want to know they did a good job or still doing a good job. You have to feel them—be precise. Insecure leaders will often ramble; uninterested leaders cut things off too quickly. Whether you are giving praise, providing constructive criticism, defining goals and dos-and-don'ts, you have to figure out how much to say and precise order. Get to the point.

7. **Be brave and honest:**
   Cowardly leaders will shy away from any number of challenging situations that may crop up or arise regularly when running a team.
   Face every situation as it is. You have to be brave and honest enough to talk to your team in a balanced and honest manner.

8. **Be a great listener:**
   Being a good and great listener is a part of a good communication. If all you want to do is talk, you are not a leader; you are probably just a boss. Keeping people motivated means listening to them, asking them questions and understanding their issues. The more you listen, the more you can respond effectively and get to the heart of things much faster.

9. **You have to know your people:**
   You don't have to be best friends or even socialize outside work, but you have to know what makes them tick. You need to know some things about their personal lives because their lives outside work matter. Their lives outside work drive a great deal

of their success (or lack of it) at work. Keep track of simple things like birthdays, marriages, children etc. The more you know your people the more common ground you are likely to find and the more you will be able to connect.

10. **Be a follower too:**
Benjamin Disraeli said, "I must follow people. Am I not their leader?" That sums up many of the other points so beautifully. Great leaders are followers too. If you are a leader but you don't follow, you are a dictator. As fun as that sounds . . . . Being a leader—follower means finding value in your team, getting inspired by your team, encouraging your team to communicate, brainstorm and be open. Very few people are great leaders overnight. It takes time and practice. As long as you are open about learning along the way and working with your team on leadership versus dictating to them, most people will be happy to go on the journey with you.

Chapter Four

PLANNING YOUR OUTFIT:

You naturally need to plan your business sustainability, growth and expansion. This is of course a major priority if you have to remain in business and keep the customers. Running your outfit with no plans virtually means running a business with no vision. A business with no vision most certainly is a business that does not care to take care of its customers.

It is not just enough to set up a business outfit and expect it to run itself and take care of its customers. You always need some sort of blue print that will serve as a guide for you and your team.

Caring for your child means looking after the child's health, feeding, education and future needs. Most times you don't sit and wait for the child's needs, you plan and provide. You probably create some sort of savings account for his tuition and all. You actually work and plan how to take care of these priorities so that you will have a productive human being in your child, someone to appreciate and be proud of.

It takes planning to train our kids. So is your business outfit. It also needs good planning in order to achieve a productive business outfit to be proud of, just like a child.

When you do take care of a child and that child grows to be a good citizen, the child will care for you and appreciate all you have done. Your business outfit will also be appreciated by your customers because you do offer them their expectations and will appreciate you and keep the patronage going, taking care of you and the outfit's sustainability.

There are so many ways and methods of making your business plans. Plans should be flexible and peculiar to your vision of the business outfit. There are of course professional business plans for the large corporations and outfits, which is mostly the standard method for such outfits, but you should plan according to the type and size of outfit you have or plan on having. We all know that how "Mr. TJ" runs his affairs will be different from how "Mr. Joe" does. One man's food could be another man's poison. You are the one with the vision for the outfit, which means you have a lot of input in your business plan. Follow your vision, whatever is needed to be in your plan, put it down. Whatever and however you plan to give or serve your customers should be there. Believe in your instincts.

Plans are often different considering factors such as your target market, financial capability, product or service offerings etc.

If "Mr. Teejan" runs a tyre service outfit, for instance, and he owns the shop, his business plan will be different from "Mr. Gidado's", who pays rent for his own outfit.

The main idea behind having a business plan is to have business survival, sustainability and growth.

BUSINESS PLAN OUTLINE

Business plans usually have a standard outline of what should be included, but like mentioned earlier, every business owner has one or two or more items or objectives different from that of the other person.

The usual standard business plan could always be found or seen as follows:

(i) **Cover sheet:**

This usually serves as the title page of your business plan, which includes:

- Name, address and phone number of the company.
- Name, title, address and phone number of owner(s) corporate officers.
- Month and year your plan was prepared.
- Name of preparer.
- Copy number of plan.

(ii) **Executive Summary (or statement of purpose)**

This is the thesis statement and states business plan objectives. Use the key word approach (who, what, where, when, how, how much) to summarize the following:

- Your company (who, what, where, when).
- Who your management is and what their strengths are.
- What your objectives are and why you will be successful.

- If you need a financing, why you need it, how much you need and how you intend to repay the loan or benefit the investor.

The executive summary is usually written after you have completed your business plan, because it is a reflection of the finished plan.

(iii) **Table of Contents:**
This is a quick reference to major topics covered in your plan.

(iv) **The Organizational Plan:**
This section should include a "summary description of your business" statement followed by information on the "administrative" end of your company.

(a) Summary description of the business
Give a broad overview of the nature of your business, in a paragraph or two, telling when and why the company was formed. Then complete the summary by briefly addressing:

- Mission (projecting short and long term goals).
- Business model (describe your company's model and why it is unique to your industry).
- Strategy: (give an overview of the strategy, focusing on short and long term objectives).
- Strategic relationships (tell about any existing strategic relationships).
- SWOT Analysis (strengths, weaknesses, opportunities and threats that your company will face, both internal and external).

(b) Products or services

- If you are the manufacturer and/or wholesale distributor of a product:
  Describe your products. Tell briefly about your manufacturing process. Include information on suppliers and availability of materials.
- If you are a retailer and/or an e-tailer:
  Describe the products you sell. Include information about your sources and handling of inventory and fulfillment.
- If you produce a service:
  Describe your services. List future products or services you plan to provide.

(c) Intellectual Property:

- Address Copyrights, Trademarks and Patents
- Back up in supporting Documents with registrations, photos, diagrams etc.

(d) Location:

- Describe your projected or current location.
- Project costs associated with the location.
- Include legal agreements, utilities forecasts etc in supporting documents.
  If your location is key or important to marketing, you may need to cover it in your marketing plan.

(e) Legal Structure

- Give a description of your legal structure and why it is advantageous for your company.
- List owners and/or corporate officers describing strengths (resumes could be included).

(f) **Management**

- List the people who are (or will be) running the business.
- Describe their responsibilities and abilities.
- Project their salaries.
- (Include resumes in supporting documents).

(g) **Personnel**

- How many employees will you have in what positions?
- What are the necessary qualifications?
- How many hours will they work and at what wage?
- Project future needs for adding employees.

(h) **Accounting and legal**

- Accounting: what system will you set up for daily accounting?
- Who will you use for a tax accountant?
- Who will be responsible for periodic financial statement analysis?
- Legal: who will you retain for an attorney?

(i) **Insurance**

- What kinds of insurance will you carry (property and liability, life and health? Etc).
- What will cost and who will you use for a carrier?

(j) **Security**

- Address security in terms of inventory control and theft of information (online and off).
- Project related costs.

The Marketing Plan

The marketing plan helps you define all of the components of your marketing strategy. You will address details of your market analysis, sales, advertising and public relations campaigns. The plan should also integrate traditional (offline) programs with new media (online) strategies.

(a) Overview and goals of your marketing strategy:
This is dependent and peculiar to the nature and size of your business.

(b) Marketing analysis
- Target markets (identify with demographics, psychographics, and niche market specifics).
- Competition (describe major competitors assessing their strengths and weaknesses).
- Market Trends (Identify industry trends and customer trends).
- Market Research (describes methods of research, database analysis and results summary).

(c) Marketing Strategy
- General Description (budget % allocations on and off line with expected ROIs).
- Method of Sales and Distribution (Stores, offices, kiosks, catalogs, d/mail, website).
- Packaging (quality considerations and packaging).
- Pricing (price strategy and competitive position).
- Branding.
- Database Marketing (Personalization).
- Sales Strategies (direct sales, direct mail, email, affiliate, reciprocal and viral marketing).

- Sales incentives / Promotions (Samples, coupons, online promo, add-ons, rebates, etc).
- Advertising strategies (traditional, web/new media, long-term sponsorships).
- Public Relations (online presence, events, press releases, interviews).
- Networking (memberships and leadership positions).

(d) Customer Service

- Description of Customer Service Activities.
- Expected Outcomes of Achieving Excellence.

(e) Implementation of Marketing Strategy

- In-House Responsibilities.
- Out-Sourced Functions (advertising, public relations, marketing firms, ad networks etc.)

(f) Assessment of Marketing Effectiveness
This is to be used by existing companies after making periodic evaluations.

THE FINANCIAL DOCUMENTS

The quantitative part of your plan:

This section of the business plan is the quantitative interpretation of everything you stated in the organizational and marketing plans. Do not do this part of your plan until you have finished those two sections.

Financial documents are the records used to show past, current and projected finances. The following are the major documents you will want to include in your business plan.

The work is much easier if they are done in the order presented because they build on each other, utilizing information from the ones previously developed.

(a) Summary of financial needs:
This is needed only when seeking financing. It is usually an outline giving the following information:
- Why you are applying for financing.
- How much capital you need.

(b) Loan Fund Dispersal Statement:
This is only needed when seeking financing too. It is an outline giving the following information.
- Tell how you intend to disperse the loan funds.
- Back up your statement with supporting data.

(c) Pro forma Cash Flow Statement (Budget)
This document projects what your Business Plan means in terms of money. It shows cash inflow and outflow over a period of time and it is used for internal planning. It is of prime interest to the lender and shows how you intend to repay your loan. Cash flow statements show both how much and when cash must flow in and out of your business.

(d) Three-Year Income Projection
A Pro Forma Income P&L (Income) statement showing projections for your company for the next three years. Use the revenue and expense totals from the Pro Forma Cash Flow Statement for the 1st year's figures and project for the next two years according to expected economic and industry trends.

(e) Projected Balance Sheet

This is the projection of Assets, Liabilities, and Net worth of your company at the end of next fiscal year.

(f) Break-Even Analysis

The breakeven point is the point at which a company's expenses exactly match the sales or service volume. It can be expressed in:

(i) Total cash or revenue exactly offset by total expenses, or

(ii) Total units of production (cost of which exactly equals the income derived by their sales).

This analysis can be done either mathematically or graphically. Revenue and expense figures are drawn from the three-year income projection.

Please note that the items to be listed below are actual performance (historical) statements, because they reflect the activity of your business in the past.

- If your business is new and has not yet begun operations: the financial section of your plan will end here and you may add a personal financial history.
- If yours is an established business: you will include the following actual performance statements:

(g) Profit and Loss Statement (Income Statement):

This shows your business financial activity over a period of time (monthly, annually). It is a moving picture showing what has happened in your business and is an excellent tool for assessing your business.

(h) Balance Sheet:

This shows the condition of the business as of a fixed date. It is a picture of your outfit's financial condition at a particular moment and will show you whether your financial position is strong or weak. It is usually done at the close of an accounting period. It usually contains:

(i) Assets.

(ii) Liabilities, and

(iii) Net worth.

(i) Financial Statement Analysis:

In this section, you will use your income statements and balance sheets to develop a study of relationships and comparisons of:

(i) Items in a single year's financial statement.

(ii) Comparative financial statements for a period of time, or

(iii) Your statements with those of other businesses. Measures are expressed as ratios or percentages that can be used to compare your business with industry standards.

If you are seeking a lender or investor, ratio analysis as compared to industry standards will be especially critical in determining whether or not the loan or venture funds are justified.

- Liquid Analysis (Networking capital, current ratio, quick ratio).
- Profitability analysis (gross profit margin, operating profit margin, net profit margin).
- Debt Ratios (debt to assets, debt to equity).
- Measures of investment (return on investment).

- Vertical financial statement analysis (shows relationship of components in a single financial statement).
- Horizontal financial statement analysis (percentage analysis of the increases and decreases in the items on comparative financial statement).

(j) Business Financial History
This is a summary of financial information about your company from its start to the present. The business financial history and loan application are frequently one and the same. If you have completed the rest of the financial section, you should have all of the information you need to transfer to this document.

The Supporting Documents

This section of your plan will contain all of the records that back up the statements and decisions made in the three main parts of your business plan. The most common supporting documents are:

(a) Personal Resumes
This includes resumes for owners and management. A resume should be a one page document, which should include work history, education background, professional affiliations and honors, and a focus on special skills relating to the company position.

(b) Owner's Financial Statements
A statement of personal assets and liabilities. For a new business owner, this will be part of your financial section.

(c) Credit Reports
Business and personal from suppliers or wholesalers, credit bureaus and banks.

(d) Copies of leases, mortgages, purchase agreements, etc.
All agreements currently in force between your company and a leasing agency, Mortgage Company or other agency.

(e) Letters of Reference
Letters recommending you as being a reputable and reliable business person worthy of being considered a good risk. (both business and personal references).

(f) Contracts
Include all business contracts, both completed and currently in force.

(g) Other Legal Documents
All legal papers pertaining to your legal structure, proprietary rights, insurance etc limited partnership agreements, shipping contracts etc.

(h) Miscellaneous Documents
All other documents which have been referred to, but not included in the main body of the plan. (For example, location plans, demographics, competition analysis, advertising rate sheets, cost analysis etc).
Like mentioned earlier, your business plan should reflect your objectives and vision for your outfit.
Most professional business plans that include the whole outline discussed above could be used for

lending or attracting an investor. If you are not targeting any of this two, it is best you remove what you do not need and tailor it to your specification, because it will work better for you.

In fact some believe that only you can determine what is needed in your plan because you are the visionary.

The Top 10 Business Plan Mistakes

Berry (2012) opined some top ten mistakes people make when writing a business plan for their outfit. These are:

(1) **Misunderstanding the purpose:**

It is the planning that matters, not just the document. You engage in planning your business because planning becomes management. Planning is a process of setting goals and establishing specific measures of progress, then tracking your progress and following up with course corrections. The plan itself is just the first step; it is reviewed and revised often. Do not even print it unless you absolutely have to. Leave it on a digital network instead.

(2) **Doing it in one big push:**

Do it in pieces and steps: The plan is a set of connected modules, like blocks. Start anywhere and get going. Do the part that interests you most, or the part that provides the most immediate benefit. That might be strategy, concepts, target markets, business offerings, projections, mantra, vision, whatever . . . just get going.

(3) **Finishing your plan:**
If your plan is done, then your business is done. The most recent version is just a snapshot of what the plan was then. It should always be alive and changing assumptions.

(4) **Hiding your plan from your team:**
It is a management tool. Use common sense about what you share with everybody on your team, keeping some information, such as individual salaries, confidential. But do share the goals and measurements, using the planning to build team spirit and peer collaboration. That does not mean sharing the plan with outsiders, except when you have to, such as when seeking capital.

(5) **Confusing cash with profits:**
There is a huge difference between the two. Waiting for customers to pay can cripple your financial situation without affecting your profits. Loading your inventory absorbs money without changing profits. Profits are an accounting concept; cash is money in the bank. You don't pay your bills with profits.

(6) **Diluting your priorities:**
A plan that stresses three or four priorities is a plan with focus and power. People can understand three or four main points. A plan that lists 20 priorities does not really have any.

(7) **Overhauling the business idea:**
What gives an idea value is not the idea itself but the business that is built on it. It takes employees

showing up every morning, phone calls being answered, products being built, ordered and shipped, services being rendered, and customers paying their bills to make an idea a business. Either write a business plan that shows you building a business around that great idea, or forget it. An idea alone does not make a great business.

(8) **Fudging the details in the first 12 months:**
By details, I mean your financials, milestones, responsibilities and deadlines. Cash flow is most important, but you also need lots of details when it comes to assigning tasks to people, setting dates, and specifying what is supposed to happen and who is supposed to make it happen. These details really matter. A business plan is wasted without them.

(9) **Sweating the details for the later years:**
This is about planning, not accounting. As important as monthly details are in the beginning, they become a waste of time later on. How can you project monthly cash flow for three years from now when your sales forecast is so uncertain? Sure, you can plan in 5, 10 or 20 year horizons in the major conceptual text, but you can't plan in monthly detail past the first year. Nobody expects it and nobody believes it.

(10) **Making absurd forecasts:**
Nobody believes absurdly high "hockey stick" sales projections and forecasting usually high profitability usually means you don't have a realistic understanding of expenses.

Business Plan is a Business Necessity

Some people always and often assume that you only need a business plan only when seeking funding. This makes a business plan sound like a fund raising tool only. A business plan is much more than that: it is a tool for understanding how your business is put together. It helps you stay focused on your vision for the outfit. It is used to monitor progress, hold you accountable and control the business's fate. It can also serve as a sales and recruiting tool for courting key employees or future investors.

Writing out your business plan forces you to review everything at once: your value proposition, marking assumptions, operations plan, and financial plan and staffing plan. You will end up spotting connections you otherwise would have missed. For instance, if your marketing plan projects 10,000 customers by year two and your staffing plan provides for two sales people, that forces you to ask yourself: How can two sales people generate 10,000 customers? The answer might lead you to conclude that forming partnerships, targeting distributors and concentrating on bulk sales to large companies may be your tactics.

As part of your operational plan, you will lay out major marketing and operational milestones. When you are the founder, the only person holding you accountable to those results on a daily basis is you. So your plan becomes a baseline for monitoring your progress. If your prototype was to be complete by July 12, and it gets done two weeks earlier than that, for example—you can ask yourself why. Was there an unexpected breakthrough? Did someone put in a heroic effort? Or did you just overestimate? What you learn will help you do even a better job next time.

But even more than a tool for after-the-fact learning, a plan is how you drive the future. All governments, for instance, drive through a plan. You don't see countries being run without a plan, so is your business. When you write, "we expect 100 customers by the end of one year, "it is not a passive prediction—you don't just wait for the customers to show up. It becomes your sales force's goal. The plan lays out targets in all major areas: sales, expense items, hiring positions and financing goals. Once laid out, the targets become performance goals.

A well written plan at anytime can be great for attracting talent. When a prospect asks to understand your business, you can easily and confidently hand them a plan that gives them an overview. Their reactions would tell you something about how quickly and thoroughly they can think through your business's key issues. The written record of your goals coupled with a track record of delivering against those goals sends a message loud and clear: you understand your business and can deliver the results you promise. Great employees will respond to that message—as will banks and investors the next time you need to raise money.

So the truth is, viewing your plan as a fund-raising tool is just the beginning of the story. You will use the plan for so much more—for managing yourself, for operating the business and for recruiting. Before deciding to skip your planning phase, consider all the implications and what they mean for your future success.

Chapter Five

YOUR STAFF: YOUR FAMILY

> *"The same way you have problems in life and have to make ends meet is the same way your staff do. They are as human as you, so treat them as such. You can't succeed without them."*
>
> —Ahmed Shehu Awak, PhD.

All business outfits set up have to be run by people. No outfit can exist without one or two or more people that will get the job done. A person cannot run an outfit all by himself/herself. You will need people with the right set of skills to form your team and make the outfit a success, alive.

The people you employ are there for a purpose too: to make ends meet in life. They are people with needs and wants. They have to feed, clothe, pay rent, go to a hospital when the need arise, attend a meeting at their kids' schools, attend friends' weddings etc. They all have a life just like you, the business owner. In essence, you have to look upon them as human beings that are with you to help you achieve your objectives and goals, which means your objectives and goals are theirs too. They are part of your business life, which makes them an important part of you.

The first mistake you can make is when you view them as your working tools. That is the beginning of dissatisfaction in them. When you tie them down on the strict rules of your organization, with no flexibility and consideration of their personal needs and life outside the workplace, things may go wrong for you. They will care less about the health of your outfit.

You need to always remember and have it in mind that your business will not exist without them and their morale on the job will be a direct manifestation on the customers.

Kaizer Plastic Products Company Limited

Mr. Kaizer is the Managing Director of his family owned plastic products company, in Kano city, Nigeria. The company manufactures plastic products ranging from toys, chairs, mats, bins and a lot more.

A master's degree holder in business administration, with a full grasp and experience in the business, having taken over from his old aged father, a shrewd business man with no compromise for his profits. He runs the business with an iron fist and books are always on the profit side.

However, Mr. Kaizer, secretly called "Hitler" by his employees have some personality issues, when it comes to his relationship with the employees.

Right from the security guard, when driving into the factory, you have to open the gates while he is 50 meters to destination and if you don't and wait till he gets there, you are in for a rain of insults.

His policy is "do as directed". He feels and acts like he knows it all. If a staff has a domestic problem and needs some time off his work hours, it is calculated from his earnings and deducted on pay day. If you are a few minutes late in "clocking-in", it will be deducted on pay day. If you are late in "clocking-out", that's your cup of tea, just be on time strictly. He has the belief that there are so many people out there looking for your job, so just do it or get fired.

This attitude created a huge barrier between him and his employees. No one feels obligated to bring up a suggestion regarding the welfare of the company. Everyone ignores problems with the belief that your suggestion don't count.

Mr. Kaizer, one day, for his own personal convenience decided to shift forward the company's break time from 12:30pm-1:30pm to 1:30pm to 2:30pm.

A few months passed by and Mr. Kaizer noticed a drop in sales. Worried over it, he inspected all departments and discovered that everything was intact. He tried figuring out the problem but just could not.

He ordered for a general meeting of all staff, after meetings with managers and supervisors failed to produce results.

Now, to his surprise at the general meeting, it was one of the security guards that stood up and mentioned a problem. The security guard stated that most of the customers preferred the initial break time because the new break time was their (customers) most preferred time of purchase. So they are all slowly opting out to other companies. The security guard said he overheard a few customers lamenting over the issue and even added that they know the boss here does not listen to anyone.

Mr. Kaizer was shocked and surprised. He then suddenly realized a lot of mistakes he has been making. He thanked the security guard and changed the break time immediately and promised further changes. He suggested everyone should write how he/she feels about the outfit and possible suggestions. He asked the letters to be without names. He was shocked and surprised to see all his lapses mentioned. He followed the entire issues one after the other and made changes in the company. He introduced a departmental suggestion box for all departments and suggestions should be anonymous.

This improved the well being of the company and he gained a lot of knowledge through this exercise. He realized he almost lost out and became a better boss. The nick name "Hitler" slowly disappeared after a few years.

This is a well taught lesson for anyone acting as the boss and ignoring that he/she works with human beings not machines and tools.

Treating Your Staff Well

As an owner of a business outfit or as the management of an organization of any sort, this is the "Golden rule" for a successful organization.

Your staff, team or employees, whichever word you choose to refer to them, is your most important asset ever in your business life. You should look at them as an "extended family" of yours.

* Appreciate them
* Seek with them

* Honor them
* Respect them
* Know them
* Feel them
* Make them feel secure
* Grow with them
* Be part of them
* Trust them
* Be honest with them

Treating them as human beings is the most successful path to a healthy outfit. Emphasis is made here on the word "outfit" because the golden rule applies to all organizations in all industries: public and private sectors. It is not a rule for the business owners only. Everyone benefits from it.

The realization that they are the wheel of success for any outfit is top priority policy. Their lives and what happens in it affects their productivity at the work place. Ignoring their lives and focusing on their work life strictly is like starting a house from the roof instead of a foundation.

Lear (2012) wrote:

"These aren't worker bees. They are individuals with human needs and desires. Appreciate those and you can make your company stronger".

From the mid 1980s to early 2000s, my world was about creating and delivering training to customer—facing professionals from high-tech blue-chip companies. For those 12 years, I witnessed firsthand a wide variety of work cultures and attitudes about team and company performance. Even though the training was in the realms of skills, knowledge and process, in the end, it wasn't as much about learning software or tools as it was about learning how to create strong personal as well as company-to-company relationships.

Since diving into the venture—backed start-up world as CEO of get satisfaction, I have had to shake myself out of some of my preconceived notions about people, performance, and the role both play in hyper-business growth.

As Deloitte's John Hages wrote in Forbes recently:

"The biggest challenge for businesses today is learning to think about their employees the way they think about their customers. How do you engage them? And on the topic of innovation, how do you apply leading practices from the cutting edge of consumer engagement that centers on human experience?

Treat your employees the way you treat your customers? Engage them just like you would your top clients? Well that's a topic I know little something about.

Bring Your Whole Self to Work:

If you want to truly engage your employees, the No. 1 thing to remember is that personal needs trump professional aspirations—every time. People wake up as human beings, not as employees. Even though many of their waking hours are spent at work, the social web and smart phones keep employees connected to their personal goals, problems and needs 24 hours a day. Yes they are always on-toggling back and forth through multiple activity streams in multiple corners of their screen.

It is true that a lot of individuals start their day by signaling to their tribe (friends, fans, and followers) that they are awake, listening, noticing, expressing and sharing too via twoo, facebook, twitter, bb messenger, viber, tango, watsapp and so on.

That is especially true in the startup world. And yes, some of that curiosity is work related, but most of it is not. The key is to understand that this connection to the interpersonal sphere the whole person is a good thing. It is good for your employees and good for your business too.

When your employees are tapped into these personal channels-checking in with their friends, family, fans and other followers—their creativity and curiosity flows. This sense of self is core to who they are both personally and professionally and it means it should be taken into account when thinking about work roles and engagement.

A whole person does the job, not just half. When you see your employees as whole people, they feel appreciated and supported. They are filled with more potential motivation to excel rather than just doing the basics of what is expected.

Personal experiences lend perspective that encourages extraordinary contribution.

Get to Work by Playing

Here is an example:

The get satisfaction team played wheel of fortune at a company—wide kick off meeting, all of the answers related to company values. Instead of lecture, on corporate values and their tenets, three contestants span the wheel, guessed consonants and bought vowels. In place of a sterile slide show for each value, we had the puzzle projected on the wall, an audience cheering them on and sound effects when contestants hit Bankrupt or guessed wrong. By engaging employees in play we made learning the corporate value upon a whole range of skill sets that extend far beyond a job description (more skills = higher value).

Simply by letting employees be themselves, you increase the value of their contribution to your business. You are not just hiring a "skill set", you are hiring a whole person. That is the returns to the outfit-creating lasting value with fully engaged employees bring their whole human selves to the office every day.

All people (employees and customers) want and expect to be engaged (at many levels). If you are not making the effort to truly connect, they will find someone (or something) who will and does. Let us hope it is not your competitor.

Hall, (2012) opined:

Renowned business builders carefully watch over their employees, like a shepherd over a beloved flock. They are kind, respectful, encouraging and highly supportive. They value their team and have learned that happy employees are the key to a first-rate business. This attribute is one of the most powerful characteristics of award-winning entrepreneurs.

I am pleased to share with you a powerful business model called the "service profit chain", authored by Harvard professors. Its premise is that if leaders honor employees, profits will be the ultimate result. It is the opposite approach from leaders who have money as his or her number one goal and for whom people are dispensable.

The model focuses first and foremost, on providing high-quality service to employees as well as to customers, with financial reward as a byproduct. It is a model used by many of the world's top companies. The points and sequential steps are as follows:

- Find and hire the best person for the job.
- Provide a culture with high values and employee support systems.
- Note that happy employees take good care of customers.
- Happy customers reward the company with revenues, profits and referrals.

Conversely, consider a poor leader who hire the wrong people, promotes a vile culture, continually criticize employees and they, in turn, mistreat customers who never return to shop and tell their friends to do likewise.

Sadly we all know companies that fit this profile and these companies eventually fail.

There are several factors that have the biggest positive impact on employee happiness. The overarching sentiment is to "treat people as you would like to be treated. As I visit with employees, these good people are delighted to share what activities, values and programmes bring good cheer to them.

All want to know the company's vision, mission, strategies and tasks that will yield success and continuous employment.

They abhor a weekly change in direction. They appreciate constant communication from management, whether good or bad. They desire clarity on their specific duties and how these tasks relate to assignment of other employees.

They expect management to pay a marketable wage with benefits and provide the necessary resources to complete a project. They wish for feedback on their performance and to clearly understand a leader's expectations.

Happy employees want to feel they own their errands and have authority and responsibility to accomplish their objective. They detest a micro manager. They seek a company culture where industry is recognized, honored and rewarded. They expect an environment of trust, fairness and justice. They aspire to live a balanced life. Opportunities for continuing education and promotions are very important.

As management meets these expectations, they feel valued as employees and willing to give their effort every day of the week.

Happy employees honor customers and customers return the favor with constant patronage. They know they are respected and treated well. They tell their friends to patronize you. Money flows into the cash register, profits increase and the company grows. Everyone is happy.

Research shows there is a one-to-one correlation between happy employees and significant positive financial returns.

Year after year, management measures the happiness level of market-star employees. When it is high, profits are excellent. When morale is less than optimal, profits are lower.

In sum, caring for employees is the right and best approach from a benevolent and business point of view. Entrepreneurs who follow this model will be blessed by their associates and will also enjoy the personal satisfaction of leading a highly successful outfit.

Motivate Your Staff

Motivating people in actual sense, is far from being an exact science, because there is actually no particular formula, strategy, calculation or handbook.

In fact, motivation can be as individual as the employees who work for you. One employee may be motivated by money only. Another may appreciate personal recognition for a job well done. Still another may work harder if he/she has equity in the business.

It is actually left to you to find out what your employees want and find a way to give it to them or enable them earn it.

And of course the size of your outfit is also a factor. For instance a barber's shop with five employees is likely to perceive what motivates them directly than a car manufacturing company with staff strength of 2000 or more.

Size has a lot to do with the art of motivation. However, some basic tips may help you realize and formulate your personal motivation strategy for your employees, as outlined by Steingold (2012):

- **Decent Salary:**
  Paying a decent salary and giving generous raises can help meet your employees' material needs so that they will be motivated to keep the pay checks coming. But money is not everything. Intangible benefits, such as good working conditions and flexible hours, can also affect your employees' attitudes and help motivate them to put forth extra time and effort.

  As a small employer, you may be unable to offer many of the work life balance perks—such as job sharing and paid time off policies, which many mid-sized to large employers can use to lure workers. Still, the tried and true techniques mentioned here can help motivate your employees to work hard and well, and stay loyal for years to come.

- **Meet Emotional Needs**
  Perhaps most important in determining whether your employees will go the extra mile is how effective you are in meeting their emotional needs. Everyone has a need to be recognized and appreciated, a desire to feel that their work has meaning, and a wish to be treated with dignity and respect.

  Many people also strive to improve themselves—to learn, do more and experience personal growth. If you can tap into these basic emotional needs and help satisfy them, your employees are likely to put more energy and thought into the job.

- **Express Appreciation**
  By taking note of an employee's effort and letting the employee know when he or she is doing an especially good job, you will reinforce that behavior—and the employee is likely to repeat and build on the traits you want to encourage. The beautiful thing is that you can recognize and reward an employee's good work at little or no cost.

  Something as simple as telling an employee that he/she is doing a good job can motivate peak performance and may even make more clear to you ways you can refine and expand current work duties.

- **Give occasional Gifts:**
  You can recognize and reward excellent performance by giving a small or inexpensive gift, whatever it is that suits best, accompanied by a handwritten note of appreciation. To get extra mileage, consider having the gift delivered to the employee's home. That way, the employee will feel enhanced esteem in the eyes of a spouse, partner, children or other family members. He/she can proudly display your gift and bask in the admiration of others. And the gift will convey a clear message: "you do good work and are valued outside the house, as well as at home".

  These small gifts can also be personalized. If an employee is a fan of "New Edition" group, a collection of their entire CDs might be a suitable reward . . . Again accompanied with a note of thanks. For a sports fan, tickets do the trick. For a gourmand, you could consider a gift certificate for dinner for two at a fine restaurant. Here again, the employee's achievement can be celebrated with a friend or loved one. Also, consider a gift for the employee's child—another way for the employee to spread the good cheer.

After an employee has worked hard to complete a project or dealt with a stressful situation, you might give the employee a day or two off-with full pay, of course.

- **Communicate clearly:**
  Be clear with your employees about what you expect. Spend time showing them the ropes. Otherwise, an employee may not intuit how you want the job done.

  Good communication goes both ways. Listen to what your employees say. Listening by itself demonstrates recognition and respect. You would be surprised at ideas that will flow from them that can be put to good use and have positive effect on the business. This will also encourage your employees to come up with more viable ideas. If you show confidence in their abilities to learn and grow into the job, you will be pleased when they meet—and even exceed your expectations.

- **Allow Room for Professional Growth**
  Many employees value the chance to expand their skills and take on more responsibility. You can take

the time to teach them yourself, or send them to a workshop or seminar. Back at work, your employees will be motivated to try new skills—and your outfit will bear the benefits.

Most employees also value autonomy: being entrusted with tasks they can carry out on their own without close supervision. Your employees are sure to be motivated and strive to do well if you delegate responsible work to them.

Finally, assure your employees that nothing bad will happen if they make a mistake. Everyone who makes a decision will make mistakes now and them, and we all learn from our mistakes. Your employees are likely to be motivated and want to earn the trust that you have placed in them. But use discretion in delegating. You do not want to create a sink-or-swim situation in which one mistake spells disaster for an employee or your business.

- **Show Dignity and Respect:**
  You can and should point out any aspects of an employee's work that need improvement, but always put it in terms of the job, not the person. Personal criticism or insults will likely cause the employee to become resentful or angry.

- **Treat staff and customers equally:**
  As you work to provide more value to your customers, think also about the people who work with you-day and night-to make this happen. You want your customers to be happy? Make your

employees happy. You want your customers to be treated with some dignity, do the same with your employees. Treat your staff and customers as one person. Your staff is one person who deserves your attention, one person whose trust you want to earn.

- **Provide other Benefits:**
  Do not put a full stop at salaries only. Employees need some non-monetary and monetary benefits as well, to keep them motivated. These could be rent allowance, healthcare cover, pension, club memberships, official cars etc. These things may seem to cost a fortune, but the benefits are immeasurable in the long run.

- **Pinpoint each Employee's Personality**
  Some people love public praise; others are mortified by it and would prefer a sincere, in-person "thank you. Make sure you take this into account if you are planning a ceremony to give awards or other recognition.

- **Use Flexibility Wisely:**
  Allowing employees to telecommute some of the time or to set their own office hours can have huge benefits. It makes employees' lives more manageable—and it shows them that they are trusted. Still, as with other motivators, one size does not fit all. Some jobs simply cannot be done effectively outside the office. Some workers actually like going into the office to escape the distractions of home or to preserve a line between home and work.

- **Offer help with career goals:**
  When you ask workers what kind of work they enjoy, also ask them about what they are hoping to do in the future.

  Giving workers opportunities to build the skills and make the connections they need to get ahead in their careers will build loyalty and motivation.

- **Recognize that motivation is not always the answer:**
  If your motivation efforts are not working, it may not be your fault. Not everyone can be motivated for that particular job, "Beasley said. If an employee would really rather be doing something else, it may be best to encourage him/her to pursue something new.

- **Consider each Employee's age and life stage:**
  There are exceptions to every generalization, of course, but workers nearing the end of their careers are often less focused on the next promotion than those who are just starting to climb the corporate ladder. Young workers may also be less accustomed than older ones to waiting patiently in a job they do not find interesting.

- **Put Money in its place:**
  How well does money motivate workers? The answer is not simple. An employee who demands a raise might really be unhappy because his/her suggestions are being ignored, for example. Surveys and experts

offer different answers about how important money is, depending on how the question is phrased.

Dee Dipietro, founder and CEO of Advanced—HR Inc., described money as a "baseline": too little of it can make workers feel unappreciated and resentful". You don't want compensation working against you as a motivator", she said. "People just don't want to feel like their employer is taking advantage of them". However, motivation to work hard rarely comes solely from money. If your employees are being paid fair salaries and still seem unwilling to go the extra mile, throwing more money at them is unlikely to be the answer.

The bottom line is treat people as people, genuinely from the bottom of your heart. This is an ingredient that helps you succeed in whatever you do as a business. Your employees deserve an even better treatment because it is safer to work with friends and people who are so into you and would be willing to do anything to see your business thrive better than any other.

The best outfit to belong to is not one with a fantastic profit margin, but one that lets its staff enjoy that profit, or fame. You know they all worked hard in making it happen.

Chapter Six

Continuity

> *"Always have it in your mind that there are so many of your competitors out there that are striving to beat you and put you out of business, or you are striving to beat and take over their customers. You don't achieve that by being stagnant. You have to aspire to make your outfit better all the time or you will be left behind"*
>
> —Ahmed Shehu Awak, PhD

There is this top leading bank in Nigeria I used to patronize. A very successful bank, with fantastic ethics. Services were highly efficient and effective. When you go to the banking hall, you are treated very well, the way you expect to be treated and probably more.

It used to be a pride to be with this bank as a customer. Customers were proud and happy with its services and brought more customers to them. This went on for quite a number of years. Then suddenly, the staff started behaving like they were doing you—a customer, a favor any time you go to the bank. They have a large customer base that probably made them feel too good.

Instead of maintaining the effective customer services, it dropped. It dropped to the extent that a staff will tell you to hold on, he/she is on the phone", will talk for long, and then tell you please wait while he/she discusses unofficial issues with other staff before facing you and behaving like it's a favor being done to you.

This attitude chased so many customers away without them noticing until they realized the number of dormant accounts they had and started follow-up. It was in vain because all the ex-customers have found other banks where they are treated like people.

Now this problem boils down to two things—either the staff are no more motivated on the job or the success has overshadowed their primary ethics of putting the customer first. Something went wrong somewhere without being noticed by the management. This is not peculiar in the business world.

As a business owner or manager, you need to keep track of success and how to maintain it and make it grow not regress.

The need to constantly probe yourself and see what it is you are not doing well is of utmost priority.

Retreats with your staff in order to explore everyone's perception and suggestions could really hit it off.

In the 2012 WTA championship finals, Serena Williams after beating Maria Sharapova, did not just walk off and wave at the fans. Despite the fatigue of the intensive match, she took time and shook hands with a lot of the fans there, because she recognizes their importance in her life. That is a good continuity relationship with them. Do not let success make you lose track.

Always keep suggestion boxes for customers and staff too, with a constant check on them. You may be surprised what you will find that will be of great help to your outfit.

The moment you start to feel very comfortable with your services, then growth and continuity is becoming an enemy of your company.

Like mentioned earlier, a self probe is important to keep check of the health of your outfit, consistently. You should always ask questions like:

- Are your customers happy with your present status of services?
- Are there changes your customers would want you to make to serve them better?
- How do you demonstrate to your customers that you care about them?
- What good things would your customers say about you?
- What bad things would your customers say about you?
- If your customer was to choose a competitor, who might they choose and why?
- Why do customers choose your competitors, rather than you?
- Why do customers choose you, rather than your competitors?
- What can you do to stop losing out to your competitors?
- Do you take your customers for granted?
- What do you compete on? Your price, innovation, quality etc.

- What would your competitors say about you?
- What does your marketing say about you?
- What does your brand stand for?
- What are your short term/long term goals?
- Are you still relevant to your customers?
- What area or where do you take your customers for granted?
- Why do customers leave you?
- What do your customers want from you?
- What is the opportunity cost of losing a customer?
- How would you describe the morale in your company?
- What is the impact of morale on profits of your company?
- Why is morale important in your company?
- What motivates you to come to work each day?
- What are your personal goals and how can you achieve them through your work?
- What do you enjoy most about your work?
- What do you least enjoy about your work?
- Do all employees believe in your products or services?
- Do your customers believe in your products or services?
- Do you suffer from high staff turnover, absenteeism, low morale, and high stress levels?
- Are your employees frustrated and unhappy?
- Are you losing your best talent?
- Do you find it difficult to attract the best talent? If so, why?
- Are your products/services relevant to your customers?
- What makes your competitors superior or lesser to you?

- How could you improve your products/services?
- How do you stop work from being just a job and make it something more important for your team?
- What do you do to ensure that your 'customer' and 'staff' is kept at the center of your company?
- How do your CEO and senior management team communicate with the rest of your organization—and keep everybody up to date, and believing in the purpose of the company, and 'on message'.
- Can you identify examples of poor communication in your company? What were the consequences of this poor communication?
- What are you doing to capture the feedback of your customers and make sure it is used to improve your products and services?

These tips will help you stay constantly in touch with how and what should be done to keep your outfit in a "progress continuity gear".

These tips may not all apply to your outfit but most should. Always apply what suits your outfit best. You should always measure where you are so that improvement can follow.

When you stick to a particular comfort zone and refuse to improve your services, you will end up being left behind. Continuous innovation, Creativity and growth are a vital ingredient in sustaining your business.

Change is the most constant factor and it is usually brought about through continuous innovation, creativity and growth.

"Redford, in "enterprise mentor", outlined some really good examples. Let us read what he wrote: "I was told recently that there has been more change in the past 400 years than the past 4000.

In fact, there has been more change in the past 40 years than the past 400, and incredibly there has been more change in the past 4 years than the past 40.

Just consider how the world has changed in your lifetime.

It was not long ago that mobile phones and handheld computers didn't exist.

Now it seems just about everyone has a mobile phone.

Mobile phones have moved beyond just making phone calls to include MP3 players, streaming movies, internet, video chat, email as well as text messaging.

You have probably seen that text messaging has created a whole new language. Text messaging is a great example of 'innovation and change' in action.

Just think of the level of services mobile phones offered 10 years ago, and consider now how they will be in another 10 years.

Any company who stands still in the mobile phone world and does not innovate or change to meet the needs of their customers will soon go out of business!

What about the evolution in the motor industry? An industry which is over 100 years old, but has seen dramatic and constant change and innovation?

It only takes 5-10 years for a car to start looking outdated; any car manufacturer that does not update their models over that same period will ultimately suffer and pay a hefty price.

Customers will not buy old technology and old designs. They want new ideas and new technology, especially in these eco-friendly times.

Cars which are driven purely by petrol will start to change to meet the needs of the customers.

We have seen this already in the US, where the demand for large gas guzzlers is diminishing and smaller fuel efficient models are becoming more popular.

No matter how much you may want things to stay the same; there is no alternative to change.

You have to understand this. Standing still and doing the same as yesterday is not an option in business. Believe me, there can be no other way forward because your customers will not accept anything less.

It should be clear now that innovation, creativity and change are the only constants in business".

I will also include the banking industry. Can you clearly recall how your life was when we had no ATMs? Consider the convenience of ATMs. You could easily withdraw cash at any time of the day and night, in case of any emergency. Your master cards and Visa cards that you can use to withdraw cash anywhere you travel in the world without hassles. This has eliminated you having to carry large amounts of cash on you. You could easily pay for goods and services online with your master or visa cards as the case may be. Any bank that does not offer such services today is probably closed and shut down. No business survives without continuous innovation, creativity and change, no matter the size and nature of such an outfit.

Continuity of running your business is probably a bigger challenge than setting up the business.

Some people may run and own businesses for years, but someone suddenly comes in, opens a new outfit and takes away the customers. That person must have done his/her homework on what the customer really wants that others are not offering.

UNDERSTAND YOUR CUSTOMERS FOR CONTINUITY

It is obvious that customers are the lifeblood of any business, micro, small, medium or large! (Of course keeping in mind that your employees are part of you and the customers too). It is a key to improving your performance. Understanding and getting to know them will keep you on the track of innovation, growth, change and continuity in business. This implies that you have to get closer to them (customers).

It is only when you understand your customers that you can give them exactly what they want, when they want it, and in the way they want it. Remember, we discussed the customer matrix?

Broadly, you may do this by:

- Finding out about your customers' purchasing habits, opinions and preferences.
- Profiling individual customers and groups of customers to market more effectively and to increase sales.
- Changing the way you run your business to improve customer service.

You may claim to know your customers inside out, and you may be right. Many business outfits assume that if people are buying what they are offering (products or services), then they must have a good grasp of what their customers want and that may not simply be the case.

Even with years of accumulated knowledge, there is always room for improvement. Customer needs change over time, which is the reason for a constant self probe on your outfit in order to know the market trends and allow room for changes so as to have continuity.

When you understand your customers better, understand what they want, and are able to deliver it to them, then you have a prosperous future ahead.

Your customers are not only a good source of ideas for new products and services, but they can also be used to benchmark your performance against your competitors.

If you get to know your customers well enough, they will tell you how much you match up to your competitors. The notion of asking customers such searching questions makes many owners/managers uncomfortable. But if your relationship with a customer is close enough, they may tell you of an underlying weakness that, once fixed, may improve your outfit.

Getting close to your customers is dependent upon your sector and type of business. For example, a service company may have only a dozen customers, whereas even a small retailer may have many thousands. With a little effort, the service company can get to know all its customers really well but the retailer may never know all of its customers. Instead, it will have to learn what groups make up its customer base, and then try to understand what each group of customers like and dislike about the products it sells and the way it sells them.

There are six broad stages you need to go through to obtain accurate information about your customers and then apply it across your business:

- Collect information about your customers.
- Store that information.
- Make it usefully accessible to you and your staff.
- Analyze customer behavior.
- Use your new-found knowledge to market more effectively
- Improve and enhance the customer experience.

The information you gathered should allow you to make a number of analysis of your customer base, using:

- Demographic data-age, gender, address, income.
- Behavioral data—what they buy, where they buy it, how they pay.
- Psychographic data—beliefs, interests, opinions.

- Firmographic data—business and sector demographics.

Some businesses may find that it is a small percentage of their best customers that generate a high percentage of their profits. With a better understanding of your customers' needs, desires and self-perception, you can reward and target your most valuable customers. That does not mean neglecting the other customers, because a small customer could always become a big one at any time.

When your product or service is almost identical to that offered by other businesses, customer service could be the differentiating factor. Successful businesses know that customer service is integral to finding, keeping and satisfying customers, and therefore spend a great deal of time and energy developing the right strategy. Every business outfit should strive to have an effective and efficient customer service because it develops loyalty and continuity.

You have to note that every business type has its kind of customer service. Do not expect to offer the same kind of customer service for a coffee shop, auto-mechanic shop, bank, hotel, motel or a hospital. You have to align with the sector you belong to and strive to offer the best.

Glick—Smith, PhD (2012) posted on Harvard Business Review Comments site:

"Practice Servant Leadership" one who operates from a position of enlightened self-interest in service to others (a.k.a—pays it forward without expectation of return) will reap benefits and success far beyond those who operate from a position of "what's in it for me", no matter how many of the characteristics of indispensability you articulate".

More tips and strategies

1. **Get your people to think and act like business owners:**

   Business—owner—thinking (rather than employee thinking) has the ability to bring new life and energy to your outfit and focuses your people on the number one thing that really matters—your customers. Get your employees to answer these questions:

- What would I do if I was the owner of this business?
- What would I expect to be done if I was a customer of this company?
- Given the decision I am about to make, what impact will this have on my customer's desire to come back and buy from us again?
- What can I personally do to ensure my customers recommend my outfit to their friends, family and business associates?

2. **Invert the Pyramid:**

   Understand that business is nothing to do with what you want, but everything to do with what your customers want. In most companies, the leader is at the top of the pyramid of organization chart.

   Invert the pyramid and put your customers at the top, rather than you. Make sure every action and decision your employees make is for the long term good and benefit of your customers.

3. **Stop losing customers:**
   Research suggests that more than 60% of customers will leave your company/outfit because of a negative experience.
   That would not happen if your employees thought like business owners and put the needs and desires of your customers first, instead of their own. Get your employees to suggest ways to stop losing customers and prospects to your competitors.

4. **Understand that business is about creating belief in the eyes of your customers:**
   You need to make your customers believe in you. If they don't, they won't patronize you.
   Ask each employee to suggest five new ways to make your customers have deeper levels of belief and confidence in you.

5. **Create happy 'repeat' customers:**
   You must turn your customers into passionate fans who tell the world about you, and do your marketing for you. Get your employees to suggest five new ways they can turn unhappy customers into happy customers, and happy customers into passionate fans.

6. **Get your employees to go the extra mile for your customers:**
   You need to thrill your customers, wow them, dazzle them and give them reasons to do your word-of-mouth marketing for you.
   Get your employees to suggest five new ways they can go the extra mile for your customers.

7. **Get your employees to come up with new business growth ideas:**
   Your employees' ideas have value. Get them to start a journal and come up with at least one or two new business growth ideas each week or monthly or quarterly. Not all ideas will be winners, but by getting them to think more entrepreneurially and by valuing their input, you will soon have valuable treasure chest of new innovative and creative ideas which will help grow your business.

8. **Turn each person in your outfit into a salesperson:**
   It is not only the sales people in your company who are responsible for selling, everyone is.
   Ask each person in your outfit to identify the core benefits of your products or services, and get them to explain exactly why your customers would want to buy from you or patronize your services.

9. **Create leaders at all levels in your company/ outfit:**
   Great leaders fire up the passion in those around them. Passion is the fuel that will drive your company forward.
   Give people additional leadership responsibility in your company, and bring out the best in them.

10. **Have crystal clear goals that are programmed deep into the subconscious mind of your employees:**
    Get your people to write down the goals of your company as they currently understand them.

Take note of the level of consistency, or inconsistency in their responses.

11. **Make your goals stretch goals, aim high:**
    Revisit your goals and now make them stretch goals. Be sure to re-communicate your new goals to your entire team.

12. **Talk about cash, not profits:**
    One of the major reasons for business failure is running out of cash. Make cost and efficient savings in your company.

13. **Create a mentorship scheme:**
    Great entrepreneurs have coaches and mentors. Start a mentorship scheme. Rather than senior people mentoring people, consider reversing this. Have the younger members of your team mentor more senior people in what is happening with technology, new media or with people of their age.

14. **Create a mastermind club:**
    The result which comes from people working together in harmony on a given project can be extraordinary. Create various mastermind clubs, each with a reasonable number of members. Task each club to revisit some of the questions we have examined and see if they can come up with even more creative and profitable ideas.

15. **Celebrate Success:**
    This does not have to be expensive, but you should get your employees suggest ways to celebrate their

achievements. Keep these ideas to hand and celebrate future successes throughout the year.

16. **Embrace failure:**
    It is often said that if you are not failing, you are not trying hard enough. Failure gives you wisdom and judgment and allows you to take larger calculated risks. Ask your employees to revisit some of their recent failures and get them to suggest what they have learnt from them, what they would do differently next time and what new opportunities came out of their setbacks.

17. **Turn your people into experts:**
    Make sure your people know your services / products inside out and the benefits they offer. The more your employees know about what you sell, the more confidence they can pass on to your prospects and customers. Your customers should never know more than your employees.

18. **Get your people to know your customers, market and industry inside out:**
    The more you know about your customers, the more you can adapt and respond to their changing needs. Get your employees to focus on your customers, market and industry. Ask them to learn about your competitors and where your company fits within your overall industry sector.

19. **Develop your employees' public speaking skills:**
    Public speaking develops confidence that teams and customers will pick up on. It forces you to know your subject.

20. **Networking:**
    Great business owners are great networkers. Encourage your employees to network with other people in your industry.

21. **Get your people to take outside leadership positions in your industry:**
    Entrepreneurs and business owners are typically active in numerous trade associations, or take leadership positions in the community.
    Involvement in these clubs and associations introduces them to new ideas and different ways of thinking.
    Encourage your employees to participate in at least one community activity—and get them to identify at least one business growth idea as a result of this.

22. Never lose sight of the fact that it is your customers who pay your salary.

23. **Get your people to read books and develop themselves.**

24. **Get rid of negative energy in your company:**
    Only positive people with positive energy will make your outfit grow and create results, negative energy will bring you down.
    A bad attitude is like a virus—and if you have people in your outfit with attitude problems that don't believe in your services/products, tackle them before it affects the performance of your business.

25. **Synchronize the needs and goals of your staff with the goals of your company:**
    Your staff must want to come to work each day because they are motivated and love their work, not just because they want to pay their bills. If they are motivated and love their work, they will demonstrate greater levels of passion, innovation, creativity, customer care and as a result, generate greater revenues and profits.
    Get each of your staff to write down their own personal goals and explain how they are aligned with the wider goals of your outfit.

26. **Eliminate Complacency:**
    There is no room for complacency and taking your customers for granted, which happens a lot in so many outfits.
    Ask your people to identify five areas where they think your business has become complacent, or takes your customers for granted and take immediate action to fix these areas/issues.

27. **Team Harmony:**
    Any team that stick together and work for each other will always win.
    Ask your staff to suggest ways to create a stronger level of team harmony and give the bright ideas a chance.

28. **Have only one standard—"excellence":**
    Ask each employee to suggest several areas which do not measure up to the high standard of excellence. Take these suggestions and fix them.

29. For the love of it:

Entrepreneurs are driven by their passion for their products and services. Money only comes by giving customers what they want and understanding it is all about your customer.

Find out what your employees personally love doing and ask them how they could bring more passion to their work.

30. Always think long—term.

References

Awak, A. S. PhD (2012). Management at a Glance for Top, Middle and Lower Executives. Author House, UK.

Ben, Y (2007, April 16th). 10 Essential Business Leadership Skills. Retrieved on November 11, 2012 from http://www.istigatorblog.com

Berry, T (2012). The Top 10 Business Plan Mistakes. Retrieved on November 18, 2012 from http://www.entrepreneur.com

Business Upgrade (Electronic Version). Retrieved on October 20, 2012 from http://www.teambuildingforbusiness.com

Enterprise Mentor (Electronic Version). Retrieved on October 20, 2012 from http://www.teambuildingforbusiness.com

Feyijimi, S (2012). Hello Boss! Your Employees are your first Customers. Retrieved on December 13, 2012 from http://blog.jobberman.com

Glick-Smith, J. L., PhD (2012). Post on Harvard Business Review. Retrieved on December 17, 2012 from http://hbr.org.

Hall, A. (2012). Treat Your Employees Well and Profits with Follow. Retrieved on December 13, 2012 from http://www.standard.net

ImproveBusPerf.pdf (Electric Version). Retrieved on December 17, 2012

Inc Staff (1999). Motivating Employees. Retrieved on December 15, 2012 from http://m.inc.com

Lea, W (2012). A Better Way to Treat Your Employees. Retrieved on December 13, 2012 from http://m.inc.com

Pinson, L (2006). Out of Your Mind and Into the Marketplace. Retrieved in June, 2010 from http://www.business-plan.com

Robbins, S (2004). Why You Must have a Business Plan.

Retrieved on December 18, 2012 from http://www.entrepreneur.com

Savar, A. (2010). Complacency: The Enemy of Success. Retrieved on December 17, 2012 from http://www.entrepreneur.com

Steen, M (2007). 10 Tips for Motivating Employees. Retrieved on December 16, 2012 from http://www.hrworld.com

Steingold, S. F. Motivating Your Employees. Retrieved on December 16, 2012 from http://www.nolo.com

www.ingramcontent.com/pod-product-compliance
Lightning Source LLC
Chambersburg PA
CBHW022106170526
45157CB00004B/1512

* 9 7 8 1 4 8 1 7 9 7 2 1 4 *